FRANKLIN PARK PUBLIC LIBRARY
FRANKLIN PARK, IL.

Each borrower is held responsible for all library
material drawn on his card and for fines accruing on
the same. No material will be issued until such fine
has been paid.

All injuries to library material beyond reasonable
wear and all losses shall be made good to the
satisfaction of the Librarian.

Replacement costs will be
billed after 42 days overdue.

FRANKLIN PARK LIBRARY
FRANKLIN PARK, IL

Guess What

FRANKLIN PARK LIBRARY
FRANKLIN PARK, IL

Published in the United States of America by
Cherry Lake Publishing
Ann Arbor, Michigan
www.cherrylakepublishing.com

Content Adviser: Susan Heinrichs Gray
Reading Adviser: Marla Conn MS, Ed., Literacy specialist, Read-Ability, Inc.
Book Designer: Felicia Macheske

Photo Credits: © Christian Musat/Shutterstock.com, cover; © Sanit Fuangnakhon/Shutterstock.com, 1, 4; © studio2013/
Shutterstock.com, 3; © Tawin Mukdharakosa/Shutterstock.com, 7; © apple2499/Shutterstock.com, 8; © GUDKOV ANDREY/
Shutterstock.com, 11; © Terence/Shutterstock.com, 12; © Ngiris/Shutterstock.com, 15; © Maksim Fesenko/Shutterstock.com, 17;
© Alla Berlezova/Shutterstock.com, 18; © Christian Musat/Shutterstock.com, 21; © Andrey_Kuzmin/Shutterstock.com, back cover;
© Eric Isselee/Shutterstock.com, back cover

Copyright © 2017 by Cherry Lake Publishing
All rights reserved. No part of this book may be reproduced or utilized in any
form or by any means without written permission from the publisher.

Library of Congress Cataloging-in-Publication Data

Names: Macheske, Felicia, author.
Title: Hefty hulks : rhinoceros / Felicia Macheske.
Other titles: Rhinoceros | Guess what (Cherry Lake Publishing)
Description: Ann Arbor, MI : Cherry Lake Publishing, [2017] | Series: Guess
 what | Audience: K to grade 3.
Identifiers: LCCN 2016029426| ISBN 9781634721691 (hardcover) | ISBN
 9781634723015 (pbk.) | ISBN 9781634722353 (pdf) | ISBN 9781634723671 (ebook)
Subjects: LCSH: Rhinoceroses—Juvenile literature. | Children's questions and answers.
Classification: LCC QL737.U63 M33 2017 | DDC 599.66/8—dc23
LC record available at https://lccn.loc.gov/2016029426

Cherry Lake Publishing would like to acknowledge the work of The Partnership for 21st Century Skills.
Please visit *www.p21.org* for more information.

Printed in the United States of America
Corporate Graphics

(READER)
J 599.668
MAC
447-2703

Table of Contents

I have small eyes that don't see well.

I have good hearing.

7

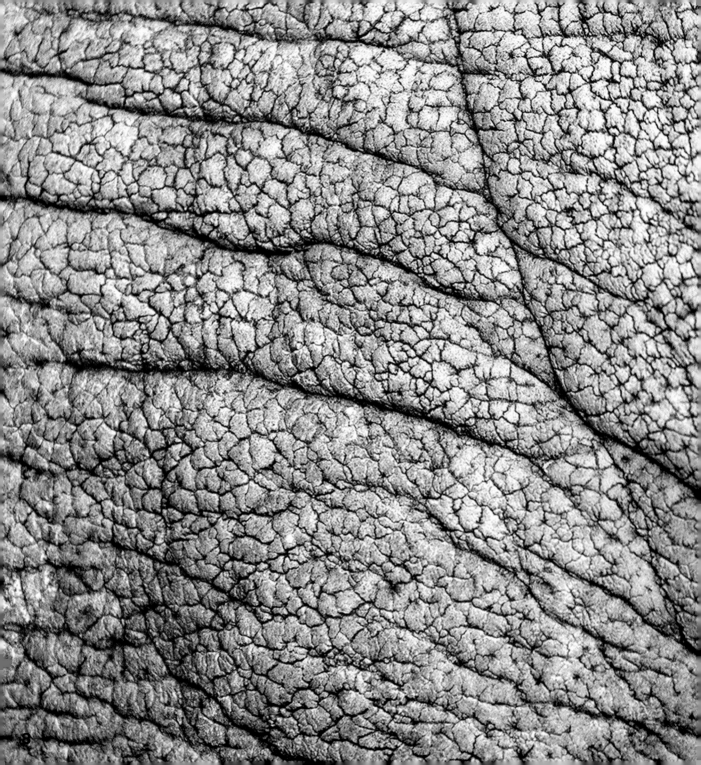

I have very thick skin to protect me.

I like to roll in the mud.

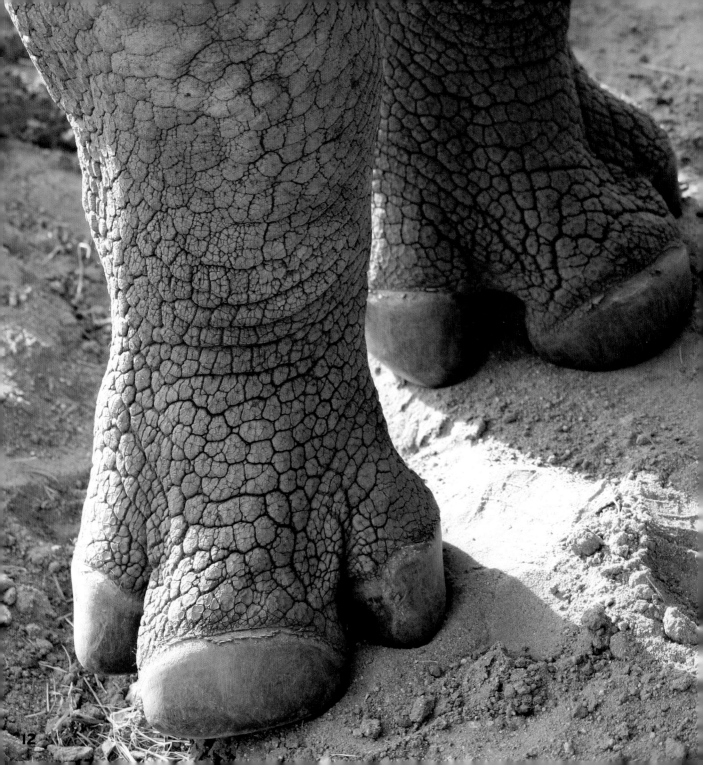

I have three toes on my big feet.

I am very big,
but I can
run fast.

WATCH OUT!

I eat a lot of plants.

I have a horn or two on my snout.

Do you know what I am?

I'm a Rhinoceros!

About Rhinoceroses

1. The word *rhinoceros* means "nose horn" in **Greek**.

2. Rhinoceroses will **charge** at things that surprise them.

3. A rhino's horn is made of a **material** that is like our hair and fingernails. The material is called keratin.

4. There are five different kinds of rhinoceroses. Three of these are **endangered**.

5. A group of rhinoceroses is called a herd or a crash.

Glossary

charge (CHAHRJ) to rush at something to fight it

endangered (en-DAYN-jurd) in danger of dying out because of human activity

Greek (GREEK) the language spoken by people who live in the country of Greece

material (muh-TEER-ee-uhl) what something is made of

protect (proh-TEKT) to keep someone or something from getting hurt

snout (SNOUT) the long front part of an animal's head that includes its nose and mouth

Index